Chelsea's New Beginning
Written by Daniel Keith Austin
Illustrated by Melissa Nettleship

Copyright © 2019 Daniel Keith Austin

All rights reserved. No part of this book may be reproduced, stored, or transmitted by any means–whether auditory, graphic, mechanical, or electronic–without written permission from the author, except in the case of brief excerpts used in critical articles and reviews. Unauthorized reproduction of any part of this work is illegal and is punishable by law.

Second Edition

ISBN: 978-1-961189-62-1 (digital)
ISBN: 978-1-961189-63-8 (paperback)
ISBN: 978-1-961189-64-5 (hardcover)

Library of Congress Control Number: 2019916559

Because of the dynamic nature of the Internet, any web addresses or links contained in this book may have changed since publication and may no longer be valid. The views expressed in this work are solely those of the author and do not necessarily reflect the views of the publisher, and the publisher hereby disclaims any responsibility for them.

Any people depicted in stock imagery provided by Getty Images are models, and such images are being used for illustrative purposes only.
Certain stock imagery © Getty Images.

Interior Image Credit: Melissa Nettleship

Lulu Publishing Services rev. date: 10/23/2019

This book is dedicated to Chelsea, the most obedient dog
that never went through formal training but always
knew how to obey commands out of love.
She was one in a million – faithful, loyal, and a friend forever.

The big sun rose over a huge field. It was a magnificent, joyous day for playing outside. A small house sat next to the field, and it wasn't long before seven Golden Retriever puppies came sprinting out. They raced through the field, playing and pulling each other's tails and ears. The puppies were beside themselves with ecstasy as they felt the sun and wind on them. They each wore different-colored collars around their necks.

A pink-collared puppy chased after her wrestling brothers, yapping, "Hey! Let me join you guys!"

Despite being ignored, she refused to give up and pinned one of them down.

"I got you! I got you!" she wagged her tail, biting her brother's ear.

Her brother shrugged her off. "You got me just this once. It's no big deal!"

As they played, a bell rang, signaling breakfast time. The puppies quickly scampered toward the source.

"I smell chicken! I hope there's plenty for me!" exclaimed a sister wearing a red collar.

"I'm so hungry I could eat a whale – with chicken!" chimed in a brother sporting a gray collar.

"Me too!" added a brother bearing a black collar. "But what's a whale?"

The puppies darted towards a rectangular patch on the field where a woman was setting out seven clean plastic bowls filled with puppy kibble, topped with chicken pieces. A water trough sat next to it.

"Eat up, puppies! We have to get moving!" the woman urged.

The woman took each puppy to a pen in the backyard. They looked at each other, puzzled by the new surroundings.

"What's going on, guys?" asked the inquisitive sister in the pink collar. "This is weird."

"Maybe she's bringing us some treats!" suggested the black-collared brother.

"Or a toy for tug-o-war!" said the green-collared brother. "Or a big meaty bone!"

"Pfft, that's silly," said the cynical sister with the purple collar. "Why would she put us in here for that?"

"We can dream, can't we?" the brother in the green collar grinned hopefully.

Before long, strangers approached the pen, making the puppies nervous. But when they saw children with the strangers, the puppies became calm. One by one, each puppy was taken away by a different person or family.

A young man and woman picked up the pink-collared curious puppy. They seemed kind enough, but she couldn't help but feel perplexed. Who were they? Where were they taking her? Would she ever see her mother, brothers or sisters again? Why were they calling her Sedona?

"What are you doing? Where are you taking me?" she whimpered. She yipped as they carried her.

But they couldn't understand her. The puppy realized that humans could never understand her or her family.

Before she could say anything to her siblings, the family carried her towards a huge metal object that she had never seen before. They opened the door and gently set her down into a leather seat. The inquisitive, curious puppy pulled in a deep breath and continued to watch the faces of the people in the object she entered.

She thought her surprise was over until the big machine started moving.

A moving house? Her eyes glowed as she watched the trees outside. This was her first time inside a car. It was just the beginning of all the things that were to come.

As they pulled up to a house, the puppy could hear the sound of children's laughter. The woman carefully lifted her out of the car and carried her towards a group of boys and girls gathered around a table piled high with gifts. The puppy's nose caught a whiff of chocolate cake in the air.

"Happy birthday, darling!" the woman exclaimed, placing the puppy in front of one of the boys. The boy barely glanced at the puppy before returning to the pile of presents. One of his friends picked up the puppy, murmuring over her cuteness.

The puppy looked up at the boy, hoping for some affection, but he simply turned his back on her and went back to playing with his new toys. The woman's smile faded.

"Are you sure you want to keep her?" she asked her son. "Taking care of a puppy is a big responsibility."

"Of course I want to keep her," the boy snapped. "She's mine now, isn't she?"

Over the next few weeks, the puppy followed the boy around constantly. She would often meet him outside his room, bowing on her two front paws and wagging her tail.

"Hey buddy, why don't you come play with me?" the puppy would bark.

The boy wouldn't even look at her as he walked past.

"I don't have time for you, go bother someone else," the boy would snap.

The puppy followed him around constantly, but the boy refused to acknowledge her. She would whine and bark for attention, but he would shut the door on her before she could come in and cuddle. As time passed, the puppy's determination to befriend the boy grew stronger.

"Please play with me! I promise I'll be good!" she pleaded. But the boy continued to ignore her, spending all his time with his friends or glued to the big television screen in his room.

One afternoon, the puppy approached the man and woman, who were watching TV, and wagged her tail.

"Let's play!" she barked.

The man tossed her a ball, and she eagerly chased after it.

This is fun, she thought.

But after a few throws, the man and woman turned their attention back to the TV.

"Hey, why did you stop playing with me?" she whined.

The man didn't seem to hear her. The puppy felt a knot form in her stomach.

"I guess they don't like me," she muttered to herself. "They'd rather stare at that stupid box than spend time with me."

She let out a sad whimper and walked away, feeling unwanted and alone.

One day, as the boy sat playing video games in his room, the puppy wandered in and sat next to him, watching with curiosity. The boy continued to focus on the game, ignoring the puppy's presence.

Undeterred, the puppy rested her head on the boy's lap, but he pushed her away. She then tried licking his hands, but he recoiled in disgust.

"Ew, stop that! Go away," he snapped, shooing her off.

The puppy cocked her head, puzzled by the boy's reaction. As she observed him playing, she couldn't understand the appeal of the gadget he held in his hands.

What is so fascinating about that thing? It doesn't even play with him back, she wondered to herself.

The puppy watched the boy for a moment longer, then decided to take action.

"Hey, let's play together!" she barked, wagging her tail.

The boy ignored her and kept his eyes fixed on the TV screen. The puppy inched closer to him and pawed at his arm.

"Come on, let's do something fun!" she yipped.

"Get off me, dog!" the boy grumbled, pushing her away.

But the puppy was persistent. She barked and nipped at his sleeve until he finally looked at her.

"What do you want?" he asked irritably.

The puppy wagged her tail and looked up at him expectantly.

"I want to play!" she barked.

Suddenly, the puppy sprang forward and grabbed the boy's controller in her teeth.

"Hey, give that back!" the boy shouted, reaching for the controller.

But the puppy was already sprinting out of the room with the controller clamped firmly in her jaws.

"Come on, let's play chase!" she barked over her shoulder.

The boy growled in frustration as he pursued the puppy down the stairs.

At the bottom of the stairs, the puppy darted between the couch and the TV with the controller in her mouth. The boy grabbed and yanked the cord, but the puppy playfully growled and held on.

"Drop it! You'll ruin it!" the boy yelled.

As they tugged back and forth, the cord snapped. The boy managed to pry the controller out of the puppy's mouth, but it was covered in bite marks and some buttons were stuck inside.

"This is just fantastic! You ruined my game, and I can't even play it now!" the boy shrieked angrily. He thrust the controller on the floor. "You're a stupid dog! I wish Mom and Dad never brought you here!"

The boy's outburst astonished his parents who had been observing the scene. They exchanged a worried glance as their son stormed off. "I don't think he's ready for a pet," said the mother.

"I agree," replied the father. "Maybe we should find a new home for the puppy."

The mother sighed. "It's just not fair to her. She deserves a family who wants her."

They both knew it was going to be a difficult conversation with their son, but they agreed that finding a new home for the puppy was the right thing to do.

Later that evening, the family arrived at a small building that was surrounded by metal cages. The puppy heard them call it "the animal shelter." Inside the cages were dogs barking and pacing back and forth. The puppy felt uneasy. She couldn't understand why her humans brought her here.

Inside, the puppy's humans conversed with a man and lady sitting at a desk. After a while, the lady took the puppy's leash and led her to the back of the building. The echoes of barking, whimpering, and howling filled the room. The lady placed the puppy in an empty cage and left her alone for the night. The puppy couldn't sleep because of the noise and the overwhelming feeling of loneliness, something she had never experienced before.

Every day, the people in the shelter gave the puppy fresh food and water, and someone new would take her outside to play in a separate yard from the other dogs. But it just wasn't the same as having a home. The puppy struggled to sleep on the cold, hard cement floor at night, disturbed by the whining, howling, and barking of the other dogs.

Why am I here? she wondered to herself. *Did I make a serious mistake? Will I ever belong anywhere?* Her eyes wandered around the room, taking in the sad and lonely faces of the other dogs in the shelter.

Suddenly, a deep female voice interrupted her thoughts.

"Hey there, little one," the voice said.

The puppy looked up to see a black Giant Schnauzer staring at her.

"Yes?" she replied, tilting her head in curiosity.

"I know how you're feeling," the Schnauzer said. "But don't worry. You won't be stuck here for long."

The puppy's ears perked up. "How do you know that?" she asked.

The Schnauzer let out a deep sigh. "To be honest, I don't really know anything. But you're just a pup, and people love pups. You'll be out of here soon enough. Me, on the other hand, I'm old and past my prime. No one's going to want to adopt an old dog like me."

The puppy's heart sank as she looked at the Schnauzer's graying fur and tired eyes. "That's not true," she said. "Someone will want to give you a home. I just know it."

The Schnauzer managed a weak smile. "Thanks, kid. But don't worry about me. You're young, smart, and full of energy. You're going to find a great home and have an amazing life. I've had a good run myself. Now it's your turn."

The puppy's spirits lifted for the first time since arriving at the shelter. She found someone who truly understood her and whom she could confide in. "Do you really think so?" she asked the Schnauzer.

"I do," the Schnauzer replied. "What's your name, kid?"

The puppy hesitated before responding. "I don't think I have one. My mother had a name, but her human didn't give any of us names. The people who gave me up called me Sedona, and so do all the humans here, but it doesn't feel like me. I never felt like a Sedona."

"Don't worry about it," reassured the old dog. "My name has been changed several times, so I'm almost sure your next human will do the same for you. I'm sure they will give you a name that suits you well."

"What did your last human call you?" the puppy asked with genuine interest.

"Brizo," replied the Schnauzer.

"I like it!" said the puppy. "It's very unique."

"Thank you," said Brizo.

"And you know what? I think you will find a home soon too. You are such a sweet and gentle dog. I don't see how any human wouldn't want you as their new best friend," the puppy reassured the old Schnauzer.

Brizo chuckled. "You'd be surprised, kid. But I hope you're right," she said.

As the days went by, the puppy felt more hopeful. Her nightly talks with Brizo lifted her spirits and gave her something to look forward to. Although she would much rather be sleeping in a warm bed in the arms of loving humans, suddenly this place didn't seem so lonely anymore.

About five or six days later, a young man named Nathan Gilbert arrived at the shelter. He exuded a quiet calmness, and his demeanor was reserved. He appeared content, but there was a sense of melancholy in his eyes that betrayed a hidden pain. As he walked towards the front desk, the woman looked up and greeted him.

"Hello there, how can I assist you?" she asked.

"Would it be possible to give me a tour of the dog kennels?" Nathan asked politely.

"Absolutely," she replied, standing up from her chair. "Follow me this way, please."

The woman led him to the back of the shelter, introducing him to each dog in need of a loving home. Nathan's attention was drawn to the Golden Retriever puppy.

"Can you tell me more about her?" he inquired, gesturing towards the pup.

The woman met his gaze and answered, "That's Sedona. She's a relaxed puppy most of the time, but she can be playful and energetic. I'm surprised she hasn't been adopted yet since she's been here for over a week. Puppies and kittens usually get adopted quickly. She's trainable, easy to work with, and super sweet – our volunteers adore her."

Nathan paused for a moment, then spoke up. "I'd like to spend some time with Sedona."

Nathan took the excited puppy to an individual yard and let her off the lead. After a few hours of playing, she nestled into his lap and fell asleep.

"So no one has shown interest in her?" Nathan asked the woman when he brought back the puppy.

"A few families did, but none followed through," she replied. "She's very sweet and she loves to learn, so she needs someone to work with her on housebreaking, chewing, and behavior training."

"I've been training dogs all my life," Nathan said. "How does she do around other dogs? I have two others."

"She's quite friendly and wants to be everyone's friend," she replied. "In fact, she's been cozying up to the Schnauzer in the next enclosure over the past week, and they sleep together side-by-side."

"I also have three cats," Nathan stated.

"Tosh is one of our cats that does well with dogs," the woman said. " We can introduce them."

"Great, let's do that," Nathan concurred.

The puppy had never seen a cat before, and she was fascinated by Tosh who was black and white. She sniffed him keenly.

"What are you?" she whispered to him. "You don't look like a dog or smell like one."

"Of course I am not a dog. I'm a cat," Tosh replied, lifting his head with a sense of superiority.

"I see," said the puppy. "What's a cat?"

Tosh stared at her for a moment, clearly annoyed by the question.

"Well, if you must know, we cats are creatures that spend our time licking our fur to keep ourselves clean, and we enjoy a good hunt once in a while, and there's nothing better than a good, long nap," he said, stretching his body and yawning loudly.

"Do you ever play?" she asked.

"Of course, but we do everything on our own terms. Unlike dogs, who are softies and do everything someone tells them to do," he remarked with a tone of contempt.

"What's wrong with that?" the puppy wondered.

"Nothing, if you don't mind being a servant. We cats just prefer to think for ourselves and do things our own way. Humans have learned to tolerate it and accept it. After all, they know we are the ones in charge," he added with a smirk on his face.

Nathan bade farewell to the puppy, giving her a warm hug and scratching her ears before he left. As he walked away, the puppy felt a twinge of sadness and sat against the bars, lost in thought.

Brizo, who was attuned to the puppy's emotions, piped up. "He was quite fond of you – I could sense it," she remarked. "But humans rarely adopt dogs on the first visit."

The puppy perked up, hope glinting in her eyes. "So, he might come back?" she asked.

"It's possible, kid," Brizo replied, nodding. "Some humans take their time to decide. But I have a gut feeling that he'll return for you."

With that, the puppy drifted off to sleep, dreaming about Nathan's home and the new and exciting life that awaited her. She wondered if there would be other dogs or cats, or if she would be the sole furry companion. Would Nathan be a kind and affectionate owner, or would he be strict and domineering? The questions flitted through her mind as she dozed off, eagerly anticipating what the future held.

The next morning, the puppy followed her usual routine of getting fed and being taken for a walk, but her thoughts were consumed with Nathan.

When will he come back? What if he doesn't choose me? And if he does, what if I make another mistake and he brings me back here? Is there anyone out there who could love me?

Although she tried to remain hopeful, doubts kept creeping into her mind. Eventually, exhausted by her worries, she settled down for a nap.

Nathan arrived at the shelter with a matching purple rope leash and collar in hand. With a smile, he greeted the lady at the front desk, "I'm here to pick up Sedona."

"Great!" the lady responded. "I'll go get her for you."

The puppy was fast asleep and barely stirred when she heard the latch on her kennel door being opened. A gentle hand stroked her face, ears, and neck.

"Hey, pretty girl," the lady whispered with a smile. "You're going home today with that caring young man."

The puppy yawned and stood up, allowing the lady to attach the lead to her collar. As they left the kennel, the puppy cast a last glance at Brizo, who gave her a reassuring wink.

In the lobby, Nathan sat in one of the chairs, grinning from ear to ear. The puppy ran towards him, jumping onto his lap and showering him with enthusiastic licks. Nathan scratched her ears and rubbed her furry back, attaching the leash to her new collar with excitement.

"That's my girl!" Nathan exclaimed. "You're coming home with me, you know that right?"

As Nathan and the puppy embraced, the lady at the shelter watched with a smile. "Just curious," she asked, "will you keep her name?"

"No," Nathan replied. "It doesn't suit her. Sedona isn't the right fit."

"I agree," the lady said. "What name do you have in mind for her?"

Nathan took a moment to consider. "She reminds me of my Golden Retriever when I was young. They have a similar face and coat color. Her name was Chelsea, and she was the best dog I ever had. Unfortunately, we lost her when she was only four years old. I wish we could have had more time with her."

Nathan gazed at the puppy, studying her as she wagged her tail and panted with her tongue out. "Yes, I'll name you Chelsea. It's the perfect name for you, baby girl," he said, beaming at her.

Nathan cradled Chelsea in his arms and headed towards the door, bidding the shelter lady farewell. As they exited, a man several years older than Nathan entered the lobby. His eyes radiated warmth and kindness.

"Hi," he greeted the lady at the front desk with a smile. "I'm Adam Wittenberg. I own the dog daycare down the street. I checked your website and saw the black Giant Schnauzer you have here. I couldn't resist the urge to come and see her for myself."

Nathan took Chelsea for a long walk in the park before showing her the new home. Although Chelsea had been out for walks before and allowed to run around in the shelter's yard, this was different. Her short life had been limited to only three places: the house where she was born, her first owner's house, and the animal shelter. The park was a new world for her with so many sights, sounds, and smells that she couldn't believe it was real. She wondered if it was all just a dream.

After several hours of playing and bonding, Nathan and Chelsea left the park and headed towards her new home. When they finally arrived, Chelsea was in for a huge surprise. She had never imagined a place like this before. A massive house stood before them, bigger than anything she had ever seen in her short life. Chelsea's eyes were fixated on the structure - she couldn't believe how enormous it was, especially compared to the vast and open space that surrounded it.

"Are you ready to see your new home, baby girl?" Nathan asked, rubbing Chelsea's neck with both hands.

Chelsea jumped around, wagging her tail in excitement. Nathan opened the door, and Chelsea eagerly bounded inside.

    Nathan and Chelsea stepped inside the house, and a small Yorkshire Terrier rushed towards them, her eyes shining with excitement. After briefly inspecting Chelsea with cautious sniffs, the Yorkie slowly approached her.

    With a gentle wag of her wispy tail, the little dog rolled onto her back, revealing her belly to Chelsea who curiously sniffed.

    Nathan smiled and said, "Meet Lily, your new sister. She seems to like you already."

A German Shepherd approached them, but he seemed hesitant about the new visitor. He stopped about fifteen feet away from Chelsea. Excited to meet him, Chelsea pulled her leash from Nathan's hand and rushed over to greet the German Shepherd.

"Chelsea, wait," Nathan warned her as he hurried after her towards the German Shepherd.

The German Shepherd glared at Chelsea, displeased that a stranger was getting close to him without permission. He growled softly.

"Rocky, be nice," Nathan commanded sternly as he picked up Chelsea.

Rocky stopped growling, but he didn't take his eyes off Chelsea or move from his spot. He sat down and scowled at her.

"Rocky, go lay down," Nathan commanded firmly.

Reluctantly, Rocky obeyed, although he continued to stare at Chelsea. He walked into the living room and lay down on the floor next to the couch.

Nathan gave Chelsea a complete tour of the entire house, including the kitchen, living room, parlor, library, and upstairs bedroom, with Lily trailing behind them, excited to have a new playmate.

During the tour, Nathan introduced Chelsea to two cats, Ophelia, a heavy brown tabby, and George, a Flame Point Siamese, who watched her with suspicion as Nathan continued the tour.

On Nathan's bed, Chelsea met Sassy, an elderly black cat, who was sleeping soundly. Nathan allowed Chelsea to sniff Sassy under his supervision. Sassy lifted her head slowly, blinked at Chelsea, and accepted her presence. When she stood up and stretched, Chelsea noticed that she had only three legs. She was missing her left front leg.

Later that evening, Chelsea savored her first meal in her new home. Even though it didn't resemble the meals she shared with her siblings, she felt overjoyed and satisfied. It was the first time since leaving her birthplace that she felt truly welcomed and loved, and she was determined to cherish the moment.

Lily eagerly joined Chelsea at the dinner bowl, wagging her tail with excitement, while Rocky kept his distance. Following their meal, it was time for play. Nathan observed from the back porch as the two newfound best friends frolicked in the yard. Lily and Chelsea played a lively game of tag, but Rocky appeared dejected. Nathan attempted to uplift him by scratching his ears and tossing a ball, but Rocky remained unmoved.

As the day came to a close, the entire family prepared for bedtime. Nathan guided Chelsea to her freshly designated crate located next to his bed. Though Chelsea had made progress with going potty outside since her time at the shelter, she still had some way to go with her training.

As Chelsea drifted off into a slumber, Lily suddenly appeared and lay down in front of her crate.

"Welcome to your new home, Chelsea. I'm sure you'll love it here. Nathan treats us with the utmost care, and we already consider you part of the family, even Rocky. He is shy with strangers, but he will soon warm up to you. Please respect his personal space as he values his alone time," Lily assured Chelsea.

"Thank you, Lily. What about the cats?" Chelsea inquired.

"They are cats," Lily replied nonchalantly. "They are typically independent creatures, but Sassy appears to have taken a liking to you."

As Chelsea caught sight of Sassy, the three-legged feline, nestled on Nathan's bed, she asked, "Why does she have only three legs?"

Sassy's ears perked up as she replied, "When I was still a young cat, barely a year or two old, I ventured out of my home and was struck by a car. My left leg was so badly damaged that the veterinarians had to remove it. But that did not prevent me from learning how to walk once again."

"How heart-wrenching," Chelsea sympathized. "How did you manage to walk on only three legs?"

"It was a difficult journey," Sassy admitted. "I stumbled and fell many times before I finally grasped it. My previous family never found me because I had no collar. I spent some time in the hospital before being adopted by some kind humans. Nathan was just a kid at the time, but he and his family took wonderful care of me and he brought me along when he moved to this house. Now, I am used to living with a variety of animals, so do not worry about causing any disturbances around me."

As Sassy released a long yawn and drifted into slumber atop Nathan's bed, Lily too succumbed to sleep next to Chelsea. Snuggled up next to her newfound beloved sibling, Chelsea was overwhelmed with immense gratitude for the gift of a genuine and loving home.

Made in the USA
Coppell, TX
02 August 2023